RL

The border for the title page is from Robert Lawson's drawing for the title page of *Mr. Revere and I.*

ROBERT LAWSON
Illustrator

A Selection of His
Characteristic Illustrations

With Introduction and Comment by
HELEN L. JONES

☆ ☆ ☆ ☆ ☆ ☆ ☆

LITTLE, BROWN AND COMPANY

BOSTON   TORONTO

FIRST EDITION

T09/72

Acknowledgments for permission to reprint other copyrighted
illustrations by Robert Lawson are given on pages 115-117.

Library of Congress Cataloging in Publication Data

Lawson, Robert, 1892-1957.
  Robert Lawson, illustrator.

  "Books illustrated by Robert Lawson": p.
  I. Jones, Helen L. II. Title.
NC975.5.L3J6   741.64'092'4   73-129912
ISBN 0-316-472816

Published simultaneously in Canada
by Little, Brown & Company (Canada) Limited

PRINTED IN THE UNITED STATES OF AMERICA

"I say, 'Willie, be eyes for me,' and you *are* eyes for me. You tell me just how things look and the size of 'em and the colors of 'em." *Rabbit Hill*

❦ IN THIS BOOK ❧

INTRODUCING THE ARTIST

IF A CAPACITY to take infinite pains is the mark of genius, as a great brain surgeon once said, then Robert Lawson's genius is unquestionable. He took pains with each line he drew, each background he textured, each detail he represented. And he expected those who worked with him to do likewise. The type design, size, paper, presswork and binding of the books he illustrated were of deep concern to him and a failure anywhere along the line could make him ill. "I was so sick over the appearance that I couldn't bear to even write about it. The jacket and front matter were beautiful — but the rest of it; the paper, printing and reproductions were just too awful. . . . The drawings of course look terrible." *

Then a happier result: "The reproductions are just about perfect, the most delicate lines are clear, and the darks are wonderfully rich, with never a gob of blob. And I do think the touch of brown in the ink helped. They have a nice warm richness. I am especially happy over the title page which might have been engraved and lettered by Mr. Revere himself." †

It is to be hoped that the reproductions in this book would have pleased him. They include over a hundred examples of his thousands of book illustrations, with just a taste of his etchings. Each illustration is printed in the same size in which it appears in its book; the two etchings are reduced as noted.

The relatively few books Mr. Lawson illustrated in color are not represented here, since they are hardly characteristic of the great body of his work; in fact, his drawings in color usually lacked the depth and definition of those in black and white.

* Letter to editor dated April 8, 1948.   † Letter to editor dated August 16, 1953.

"We Fix Flats"

❧ 1 ❧

HOB AND OTHER GOBLINS

◄§ PURE FANTASY §►

ROBERT LAWSON'S first recorded appearance among illustrators of children's books was in *The Adventures of Little Prince Toofat* by George R. Chester, published in 1922. Far above the quality of the story they illustrated, his large full-color paintings first appeared serially in the *Delineator,* starting in June 1921. The influence of Arthur Rackham showed clearly, as it would in his later illustrations of folk and fairy tales.

The great children's book editor May Massee gave Robert Lawson his first commission as a book illustrator, choosing him to illustrate for Doubleday Doran Junior Books *The Wee Men of Ballywooden,* by Arthur Mason. This and two shorter-lived books by the same author brought the artist to the attention of other editors beginning to specialize in children's books. Bertha Gunterman at Longmans Green was responsible for his first connection with the mainstream of children's literature when she chose him to illustrate the American edition of Ella Young's stories of Ballor's Son.

In her foreword for *The Unicorn with Silver Shoes,* Ella Young wrote that Ballor's Son especially delighted her child listeners, "perhaps because he was not a model of all the seven deadly virtues." This approach was as agreeable to Robert Lawson as it was to the children. He scorned what he called "juvenile books," perhaps because of his early association with such insipidities as Little Toofat. To suggest to him, as a publisher once did, that a manuscript was being scanned by a "juvenile expert" was to cause an explosion like Ferdinand's when he sat on the bee (see pages 26 and 27). He insisted that he would draw what he liked for anyone who liked it, whether adult or child. Obviously, he liked to draw leprechauns, giants, dragons and other fantastic beings. And naturally, the people who liked these drawings best were the children, since they had even fewer grown-up inhibitions than the illustrator.

The etching on the reverse page, of Pegasus being shod by elves, was issued as the presentation print for the Society of American Etchers, 1932. This reproduction is reduced by about two inches overall, the actual size of the plate being 6⅞ by 8⅞ inches. From the Frederick R. Gardner Collection in the Free Library of Philadelphia.

". . . there, lying on his back, on a wide-spreading palm, was the Jackdaw, blowing the bagpipes."

Headpiece for chapter ten of "Cog-gelty-Curry" in *The Wee Men of Ballywooden*, combining fine pen line with solid black. The six-pointed star is accurate detail, for the wee men navigated by it.

Full page from *The Wee Men of Ballywooden*. Originally in fine pen and ink reproduced by line cut.

" 'I've known the Jackdaw when he was a well-behaved Wee Man,' said the Meadow Sniffer."

The Clan of the Bog

DAISY GATHERER • *SNEDDER* • *TURF DRYER*

4

"The Rock Cod jockeyed the Cockle Gatherer."

These drawings and that at the foot of the opposite page are in Arthur Mason's *From the Horn of the Moon.*

"The Wee Pig laughed too."

COOER · WHEELER of DAYLIGHT · THIN FINGER the FIFER ·

"The Ogre was walking very slowly — for him."

Frontispiece of *The Unicorn with Silver Shoes.*
From the story "Flower of the Moon."

"With a scream the beast stood upright."

From "Kyelins, Blue and Green" in *The Unicorn with Silver Shoes*, another reproduction of a fine pen-and-ink, somewhat overreduced.

"Three Golden Apples" from
The Unicorn with Silver Shoes

"I pulled the young whelp's nose."
The Roving Lobster by Arthur Mason

"The Goldfish" in Eleanor Farjeon's
One Foot in Fairyland

Elegant trifles in pen and ink
accented with black tempera

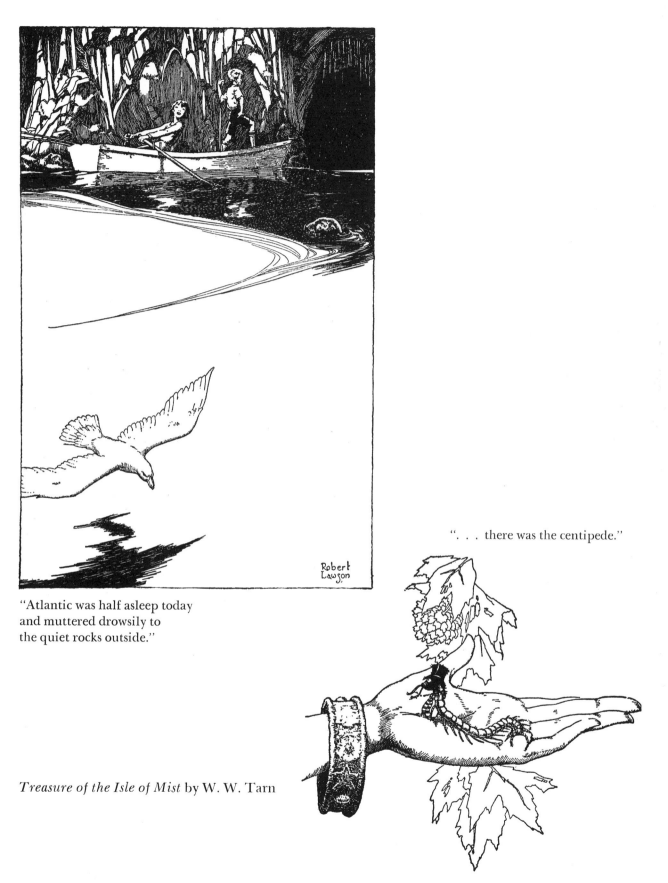

"... there was the centipede."

"Atlantic was half asleep today
and muttered drowsily to
the quiet rocks outside."

Treasure of the Isle of Mist by W. W. Tarn

9

The Hurdy-Gurdy Man ". . . strode whistling into town with his hurdy-gurdy strapped to his back." *The Hurdy-Gurdy Man* by Margery Bianco

"The children had heard him."

"... the monkey took to him amazingly, and he to the monkey."

" 'Can't I undo the spell?' said the little dragon. 'You might,' said the gypsy. 'Take a crystal bowl, fill it with powdered sea shells steeped in elderberry cordial, and drink deep. That should serve you.' " "The Little Dragon" by Constance Savcy in *Just for Fun*

Signs of the freer and heavier line which Robert Lawson used when humor broadened and jobs multiplied.

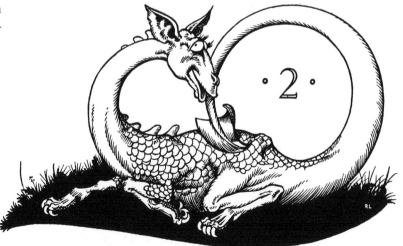

Chapter head for *Poo-Poo and the Dragons*

". . . no one could tell which was which."
The Story of Simpson and Sampson by Munro Leaf

"Even while the boys were tiny babies, anyone could see that
Simpson was very, very good and Sampson was very, very bad."

"Sir Simpson would ride forth . . . to right all the wrongs.
And Sir Sampson would ride forth to wrong all the rights."

15

16   The Two Philosophers. *The Crock of Gold* by James Stephens

"There was Ermyntrude, walking very proudly along the street pushing the baby carriage in front of her." *Poo-Poo and the Dragons* by C. S. Forester

The battle between the Remora and the Firedrake in *Prince Prigio*

This turbulent two-page spread for Lang's obscure fairy tale was a dramatic change from the ridiculous dragons of Poo-Poo. No wonder it finished the artist's association with dragons and their ilk!

"The rain, they say, is a mouse-gray horse."

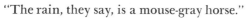

~§ 2 §~
ANIMALS TALL AND TRUE

❧ FABULOUS ANIMALS ❧

THE VIGOROUS DRAWINGS of animals which appeared wherever possible in Robert Lawson's early illustrations of fantasy indicated one of the directions his later work would take. His ease with animal symmetry is as evident as his occasional unease with the human form. And like all fabulists he often used animals to comment on human actions. Though he seldom clothed them with anything more than a hat or a stick, the human attributes he gave them sent chills down the spines of market-minded editors, who had been told that children's librarians avoided animals that talked, to say nothing of those that wore pants.

May Massee, by then at Viking, had no such timidity. She agreed to take a chance on a small piece of nonsense resulting from a collaboration between Robert Lawson and Munro Leaf. The latter had decided that his friend Lawson should do a picture book, in which the drawings would be as important as the text rather than simply an embellishment of it. So he proposed to write a story about gnomes and leprechauns and other fairy types which were then apparently the artist's favorite subjects. But when he had written it, on two sheets of paper, it turned out to be a story about a bull and, wrote Lawson later, "I had never drawn a bull in my life! So I laughed over it and told him how swell I thought it was — for someone else. After a couple of months, though, I really had to do something about it. I went to the library and got every picture and book that I could find about Spain and bulls and bullfighting. I studied Spanish landscape, Spanish architecture, bull anatomy, the costumes of Picadores, Matadores, Banderillos, their horses, trappings and private lives."

With each rough sketch the enthusiasm of author and artist grew, and so did *The Story of Ferdinand.* After its publication the stage was set for other tales that would have happened, for instance, if a penguin were shipped from the South Pole to a house painter, if a man could talk with animals, if a mole had taken an overdose of vitamins. Meanwhile the artist had become an author and some of his tales were more true than tall, such as those he wrote about the animals he knew and loved at Rabbit Hill.

Wherever in the following pages the title of a book is given without its author, RL is author as well as illustrator. The familiar initials will be used occasionally in referring to him, as they came to be by those too young or too new to use the "Rob" of his long-time associates.

The illustration on the previous page is the half-title drawing for "Animal Fancies" in *Under the Tent of the Sky,* a collection of poems about animals selected by John E. Brewton. The quotation is from a poem by Rowena Bastin Bennett.

O nce upon a time in Spain

The opening page of *The Story of Ferdinand* by Munro Leaf

A bull named Ferdinand preferred sitting peacefully
under a cork tree to brawling with the other little bulls.

". . . because she was an understanding mother, even though
she was a cow, she let him just sit there and be happy."

"He didn't look where he was sitting . . ."

26 The actual timelessness of the story was apparent.

Despite the interference with art and readability of a huge initial letter on page one; . . .

and despite, or maybe because of, the artist's use of a heavier line and less detail than heretofore; despite, maybe even because of, his caricatures of animals and men, . . .

The Story of Ferdinand became a small classic and Ferdinand himself joined the English language.

Originally printed against a yellow tint block

The Wanton Calf

Five years later came Ferdinand's sister and RL's study of bovine anatomy paid off again in *Aesop's Fables,* a new version written by Munro Leaf.

All for Aesop according to Leaf

"I love little owls."

Above and below: from *Four and Twenty Blackbirds* collected by Helen Dean Fish. Reappearance of cat at the foot of the page is in *The Little Woman Wanted Noise* by Val Teal.

RL once wrote, "I'm not too hot as a cat artist — perhaps because it is so hard to do justice to a member of one's family."

"The delighted penguin was indeed marching."
Mr. Popper's Penguins by Richard and Florence Atwater

Greta　　　First Chick　　　Captain Cook

RL's first association with an award winner occurred when *Mr. Popper's Penguins* was a runner-up for the Newbery Medal in 1939. His bold ink line for that book was marred by the addition of a harsh blue second color in the full-page drawings, but that did not prevent its acceptance with glee by generations of children.

" 'O-r-r-r-r-h, o-r-r-r-h,' he trilled."

". . . they walked to the bus line very nicely."

". . . a shower of flying tools, . . .
and the serviceman was gone."

"You almost think they're people, they act so much like us."
From "Penguins" by Anne Brewer in *Just for Fun*

"New Folks Coming!"

New indeed. The artist turned author distilled his affection for his home and its animal inhabitants into *Rabbit Hill*. "I do think it has that cozy-home and home-life atmosphere that children love in stories of animals, also very definite characters, which they also love," he wrote.*

A change in technique from pen to pencil, and superb gravure reproductions of the drawings, added even more warmth to the story which brought him the Newbery Medal in 1945.

* Letter to editor received July 27, 1943.

up DANBURY way

FAT-MAN-AT-THE-CROSSROADS

THE NORTH FIELD

THE

THE PINE WOOD

CROSSROADS

PORKEY'S HOME

Endpaper for *Rabbit Hill*

Little Georgie, Mr. Muldoon, Father, and Willie

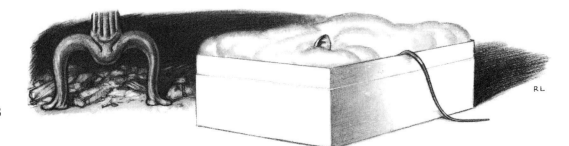

These and opposite from *Rabbit Hill*

Frontispiece for *Country Colic,* a book for adults

The other side of nature's coin,
and back to pen and ink.

Thought opposite the Table of Contents:
"When Adam delved, and Eve span,
Who was then the laundryman?"

" 'Half an hour more,' said the horse."

Mr. Wilmer: "Not strictly a juvenile book," wrote RL.

" 'How han I hawk wiv his ham hick in my mou?' "

"The only upset came when Mr. Wilmer attempted to question a Siberian Bear. . . . 'I just can't understand him,' he said. 'He keeps saying something that sounds like *Ne govoru po Angliski.*' "

RL

"Once or twice through openings in the clouds they caught glimpses of his dark form, still rising slowly, still swimming easily." *Mr. Twigg's Mistake*

Frontispiece for *Robbut: A Tale of Tails*

Pencil reproduced by offset halftone

"They flew around to the Tower and watched the Beefeaters making their rounds." *The Fabulous Flight*

Pen and ink reproduced by offset line, originally printed in a gray-black ink.

"Gus came to rest beside one of the gargoyles,
high up among the towers of Notre Dame."

RL: ". . . Peter and Gus beside the gargoyle on Notre Dame, I am quite proud of. That particular gargoyle has been done by every etcher for the past hundred years or so and I think my version stands up very well as compared to most of them." *

* Letter to editor of May 26, 1948.

Edward, Hoppy and Joe

And Their Outlandish Ideas

Pencil reproduced by offset halftone

" 'Why goodness,' he cried, 'it must be Christmas Eve!' "
The Tough Winter

RL

Frontispiece for *The Tough Winter,* the second story about the animals of Rabbit Hill

Pencil reproduced by offset halftone

". . . the Buck stamped angrily."

" 'Well, well. . . . Where is everybody?' "

M A N H A T T A N

"...they have bought the island Manhattes from the wild men for the value of sixty guilders"

From a letter of Peter Schagen, Nov. 5, 1626.   This is N° 11 of an Edition of 100 Proofs.

❦ 3 ❦

HISTORY ACCORDING TO HUMANS

←⑂ THE FLAG ⑆→

HIS COUNTRY and its history was Robert Lawson's other abiding interest. It showed early in his etchings, and even in his advertising art. His first published drawing was for a poem on the invasion of Belgium in World War I, which appeared in *Harper's Weekly* for January 30, 1915. A series of advertisements for Budweiser entitled "Framers of the Constitution of the U.S.A." ran that winter in the same magazine and more clearly foreshadowed his later work on historical subjects.

Either these examples or his drawings for a children's book, *Peik* by Barbara Ring, led Little, Brown and Company to commission him to illustrate the first book of serious fiction by John P. Marquand. His chapter-head drawings, amounting to half titles, for *Haven's End* added to its distinction and established the second of his two most fruitful publishing associations.

Besides his careful attention to period costume, RL's historical drawings continually reflect his special interests in structural detail, in tools and old guns, and in the flag. He drew the American flag of Betsy Ross and of Francis Scott Key; the flag below which Jackson toasted the Union and that before which children of his own day pledged the oath of allegiance. If these were symbols of his Americanism, so was his pride in his Confederate father and pioneer mother; so would be his willingness to poke fun at familiar historical figures.

His independent, individualistic nature made him mistrust the New Deal and all manifestations of the "welfare state." Private enterprise, his own that is, had served him well, and he saw no reason why it should not do the same for others. When he later planned a "sort of series giving the real lowdown on various historical characters," he said, "I only wish I might live long enough to see FDR in proper perspective. The present seems distinctly cockeyed."

The etching on the previous page is from the Frederick R. Gardner Collection in the Free Library of Philadelphia, reduced in this reproduction from its actual size of 11⅞ by 8⅞ inches.

Pen and ink chapter title for "The Powaw's Head," in *Haven's End* by John Marquand

" 'Man!' said Captain Swale, 'Do you dare stand before me and criticize the justice of our court?' "

Title drawing for "Tom Swale"

"It was down by the old yard where the Swales built the . . . last of the wooden ships that came out of Haven's End."

Half title in pencil and tempera for *The Golden Horseshoe,* a story of colonial Virginia by Elizabeth Coatsworth

The other illustrations for this book shown here and opposite were done in pen and ink, reduced and printed from line cuts.

". . . the great landowner in his long coat of fine broadcloth laced with gold, . . . facing the ugly little crop-headed weaver."

" 'We will see how good
an Indian you can make.' "

"Behind him came eight young men
carrying the dead stag on a litter."

" 'Boston, sir! Damn Boston!' "

" 'Them as needs shirts, take 'em!' "

From *Drums of Monmouth,* a fictionized biography
of Philip Freneau by Emma Gelders Sterne

" 'Dan Boone took eight men out
with him. . . . Two returned.''

From *Seven Beads of Wampum* by Elizabeth Gale

A story of early Manhattan

Endpaper for *They Were Strong and Good*, Caldecott Medal winner of 1941

Originally printed in an orange buff ink

"So my mother's mother sent her to a convent to go to school.
It was quiet and peaceful." *They Were Strong and Good*

"My father would sit up very stiff and hold his flag
very straight. . . ." *They Were Strong and Good*

"Don't fire until you see the whites of their eyes." *Watchwords of Liberty*

"Sir, I have not yet begun to fight!" *Watchwords of Liberty*

"O say, can you see, by the dawn's early light. . . ."

RL wrote concerning *Watchwords of Liberty*, "In selecting these I have tried to think first of two things, how familiar they are and how expressive of the real American spirit of independence. Then of their illustrative possibilities and then of how well they fit in to make a fairly continuous story of our development." *

* Letter to editor received sometime in February 1942.

"With malice toward none, with charity for all . . ."

". . . about the book of quotations, I have regarded it as a rather magnum opus, of much more importance than any books that I have done yet." *

* Letter to editor received in late September 1942.

Frontispiece for *The Great Wheel,* in which RL
told and drew a story of the Chicago Fair of 1893

"The shaft rose steadily, slowly — like the tide rising up the rocks on Kilda Point." *The Great Wheel*

"He leaned far out, held
only by his safety belt."

Above is a half-page drawing for
The Great Wheel, at the right a
much earlier drawing for *Slim*, by
William Wister Haines.

"... this endpaper, which contains a very detailed portrait
of the Ferris wheel, is taking a fearfully long time." *

* Letter to editor of March 6, 1957.

69

ERIPUIT · CŒLO · FULMEN · SCEPTRUMQUE · TIRANNIS

◄§ 4 §►

ANIMAL VERSIONS OF HISTORY

❧ THE AMOS-I VIEW ❧

WITH *Ben and Me* Robert Lawson set about to give his "real lowdown on historical characters." His "cock-eyed histories," as he called them, combined the subjects he liked best to draw and gave his imagination and humor free scope. They were nonetheless grounded in extensive research.

When an irate scholar wrote the publisher in regard to *Capt. Kidd's Cat*, "One of your editors should be hanged. Mrs. Kidd's name was Sarah Bradley Kidd, not Katherine. . . . The backgrounds of Mr. Lawson's pictures bear no resemblance to what New York looked like in 1695. Nor was Kidd a wizened, sharp-nosed skinny fellow" — the letter was referred to RL. A copy of his reply came back to the publisher carrying on the face of the envelope a drawing of the unfortunate editor hanging on a gibbet. The letter inside disposed of his critic by other means:

"In a book of this sort it is customary to clothe a skeleton of fairly well established facts with humor and imagination, expecting to find the same qualities in the reader. . . . However, the review which you have read seems to have caused some misconceptions which I hasten to set right. First, the matter of Madame Kidd's name . . . 'Katherine' seems to be entirely an invention of the reviewer. In the book she is addressed correctly as 'Sarah.' Second, in the drawings Kidd is neither skinny nor wizened. He is of small stature, yes, but stocky, husky and as ruddy as can be shown in black and white. Third, the East River waterfront view was done chiefly from Brevoort's reconstruction of Danckaert's drawings."

Gibbet in
The Crock of Gold

In closing this letter RL commented, "In the past fifteen years I have done about fifteen books. *Capt. Kidd's Cat* occupied slightly over a year; research, writing and illustrations, the latter alone taking about ten months of hard labor."

The drawing on the previous page is the frontispiece of *Ben and Me*. The Latin inscription varies slightly from that on Houdon's bust of Franklin, and is translated, "He snatched the thunderbolt from heaven, then the scepter from tyrants."

". . . I feel the time has now come for me to take pen in paw
and set things right." Head for Chapter 1 of *Ben and Me*

In October 1938 RL wrote the art director of Little, Brown: "I have
been thinking over the Famous Person and his pet idea and have sort
of boiled down to one that I think ought to work out very well — it
certainly would be a grand opportunity for drawings.

"This is the story of a mouse who took up his residence in Ben Franklin's fur cap which he always wore, and which I have always felt must
have been inhabited by *something*."

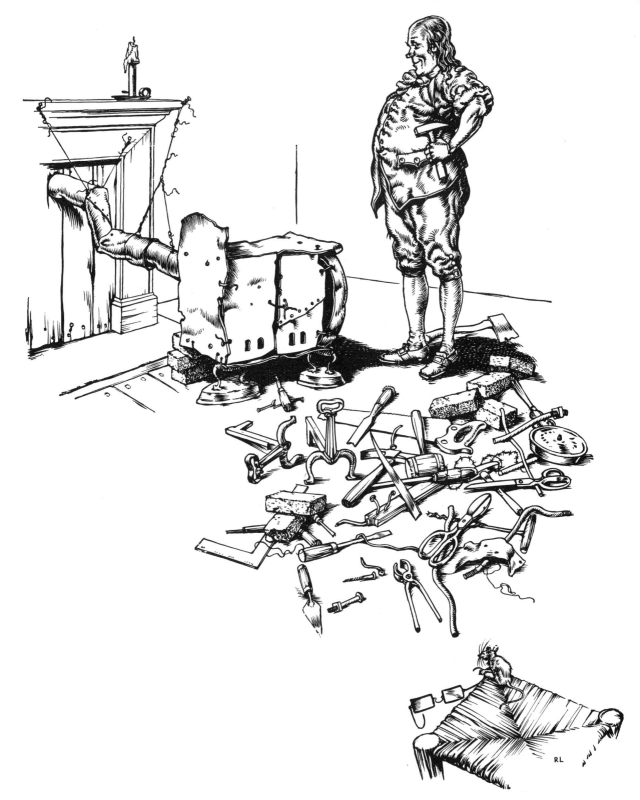

"It looked pretty promising."
Chapter 2 of *Ben and Me:* "We Invent the Franklin Stove"

"The next half-hour was the most awful experience of my life."
Chapter 8 of *Ben and Me:* "That Kite"

"A scene of the wildest confusion followed. . . . Through the window they came piling — the sailor rats of John Paul Jones. Fifty fighting Yankees! LAFAYETTE, WE ARE HERE!" *Ben and Me*

RL wrote on August 1, 1937: "The Battle of Versailles double spread is coming well, . . . There are some 45 figures so far and I have not even reached the mice or the ship rats of John Paul Jones."

Endpaper for *I Discover Columbus,*
originally printed in a blue-green ink

"I think the best bet would be a parrot."
Letter of December 8, 1939, to RL from editor

"The jungle Indians then were
a sweet and peace-loving race."

. "He was seasick!" *I Discover Columbus*

RL wrote in July 1941, "I am much excited over Paul Revere as a new subject for another cock-eyed biography." But other books as well as a lack of buyer enthusiasm for *I Discover Columbus* postponed the coming of Paul for a full ten years. Then in December of 1951, "I have gotten started on a new opus, about Paul Revere, as written by his horse."

"I fell, a clumsy sprawling fall, tossing
my poor Leftenant far over my head."

Mr. Revere and I

"Look," he said . . . , 'Paul Revere needs a horse badly.' "

" '. . . aforesaid horse is . . .
hereby expropriated for service
in the advancement of Freedom,
Equality, and Independence.' "

"They all adored me
and were in and out of
the stables continually."

Mr. Revere and I

"The harbor waters became covered
with a thick scum of sodden tea leaves."

" 'General,' Mr. Adams suggested,
'Mr. Revere is a well-known artist in teeth.' "

Warriors' Return

"Did you know that Capt. Kidd's cat, Gallagher, wore a small gold ring set with a ruby in his left ear? . . . am doing some research and taking photographs of our Blitzkrieg who, whether he likes it or not, is going to be Kidd's cat," RL announced on April 3, 1954.

Off Pearl Street, Manhattan, in Kidd's Time

". . . you could have knocked me over with a capstan bar when I saw him
. . . looking more like a country parson or a countinghouse clerk than a
seafaring man." *Capt. Kidd's Cat*

"A Real Captain, Is Kidd!" Head for Chapter 4

"He . . . gave her every gun of his port battery."

"With a good breeze we slipped through the Narrows,
and went swirling up the East River."

"St. Mary's Again." Head for Chapter 8, *Capt. Kidd's Cat*

❧ 5 ❧
PEOPLE—LARGE AND SMALL

~§ ROUNDUP §~

THOUGH ROBERT LAWSON could catch a likeness deftly when he wanted to and though different types of character intrigued him, he did not care especially to do "ordinary modern people," as he wrote in 1946. His drawings of women and children most often reflected this disinterest; sometimes they seem little more than patterns. Yet all manner of men live in his illustrations, and he worked hard to make his pictures of them say what he wanted them to.

The examples in this final section run from the sublime to the ridiculous and perhaps may be taken as a capsule measure of the limits of the artist's work. The gap between his *Pilgrim's Progress* and his *McWhinney's Jaunt* was bridged with an extraordinary production of fantastic, historical, natural, and humorous drawings. Accompanying this enormous creativity were a narrative sense and a facility with words rarely found in artists. RL is still the only man who has won both of the highest awards given to children's books in the United States: the Caldecott Medal for *They Were Strong and Good*, and the Newbery Medal for *Rabbit Hill*.

The illustration on the previous page is a full-page chapter title from *At That Time,* a book which RL defined as "a study of childhood, based somewhat on my own, written for adults."

Pilgrim

Peik

Orkney Sailor

Money Changer

Old Surly

Center from *Wind of the Vikings* by Maribelle Cormack
Upper left from *Peik* by Barbara Ring
Upper right from Bunyan's *Pilgrim's Progress*
Lower left from Farjeon's *One Foot in Fairyland*
Lower right from Bowie's *The Story of Jesus*

93

"When That Mountain Fiddle Cries." Half-title drawing for a section in *I Hear America Singing,* an anthology of folk poetry edited by Ruth Barnes. The original was printed in black and red.

Head and tail piece for section containing verse of Riley, Lowell, Field, Guest and others

"Joseph would tell stories also to the Boy."
The Story of Jesus by Walter Russell Bowie

Carpenter's tools used as a spot
in *The Story of Jesus* are similar
to those of early America.

"Wee Gillis went up into the Highlands." *Wee Gillis* by Munro Leaf

"Then he held it the way he used to
when he was stalking stags in the Highlands."

97

Frontispiece and title page spread for *Pilgrim's Progress* by John Bunyan, retold and shortened by Mary Godolphin. Pen and ink reproduced by offset line.

In his foreword to this handsome edition of a version
first published in 1884, Robert Lawson said, "As for the
illustrations, I have tried more than anything else to
make the characters living and real, with fairly accurate
costumes and surroundings of Bunyan's time. If a cer-
tain element of caricature or humor appears, seem-
ingly out of place in a book so essentially religious, I
can only say that it is there because I think John Bunyan would have wanted it that way. . . . When he de-
scribes the beauties and delights of the Promised Land
I think he would have wanted them pictured as beau-
tifully as possible and this I have sincerely tried to do."

The Valley of the Shadow of Death

The Giant Despair

Land of Beulah

A predominance of legs.

Intentionally or not, these pen and ink drawings from Eleanor Far-jeon's *One Foot in Fairyland* suggest an unconcern with the proportions of the human form.

". . . the little girl laughed. That so much pleased Adam that he stood on his head until the blood began to pound in his face." *Adam of the Road*

Elizabeth Janet Gray's story of a minstrel boy in medieval times gave RL still another association with an award winner when it won the Newbery Medal for 1943.

"... a man on horseback clattered round the curve behind them and without slackening his pace pounded down the road ahead." *Adam of the Road*

"Roger's hand was warm and strong, and Adam clung to it."
Adam of the Road by Elizabeth Janet Gray

"McKinley greeted Davy with deep though quiet pleasure." *Smeller Martin*

Although RL let the man speak in exaggerated dialect,
his portrayal of his face is by no means a stereotype.

And so on to the marvels of Z-gas, with which Robert
Lawson may have pedaled farther into the future than
he knew when he went along on *McWhinney's Jaunt.*

RL often lamented, as he finished a book, having to part with the characters in it when he shipped them off to the publisher. Similarly, the
temptation to go on choosing pictures for this one is strong, but for
practical purposes must be resisted.

VITAL STATISTICS AND
TECHNIQUES

THE FACTS about Robert Lawson's life — his birth and death and interim whereabouts — are available in various sources, including *Illustrators of Children's Books,* the original volume covering 1744 to 1945 and the supplement covering 1946 to 1956, both published by The Horn Book, Inc. So are evaluations of his work, including the paper by Mary Burns given in 1971 as the final Hewins-Melcher lecture to the New England Library Association. This book has been planned to allow individual perusers to make their own evaluations. The following information may be helpful to those who do not have other biographical sources at hand:

Robert Lawson was born in New York City on October 4, 1892. He was brought up in Montclair, New Jersey, where he went to high school. Then he studied at the New York School of Fine and Applied Art. "In the three years that I spent there," he once told an interviewer, "I learned that there was a great deal to be learned about art. . . . From 1914 to 1917 I was a Greenwich Villager and began to absorb a few things they hadn't taught in art school. My art activities were varied and pretty bad. I did some commercial drawings, illustrations for *The Delineator, Vogue,* and *Harper's Weekly* (which promptly fell dead), designed scenery and costumes for the Washington Square Players, wrote, costumed and directed a large pageant, did book plates, tried some portraits." *

When the United States entered World War I, Lawson joined the camouflage section of the Army and spent two years in France. On his return he moved from New York to Westport, Connecticut, where he spent the next ten years doing commercial art for posters and advertisements, magazine illustration, and greeting cards. In 1922 he married Marie Abrams, also an illustrator and author. Together they purchased the house and land in Westport which they called Rabbit Hill, and set out to pay for it by designing a greeting card apiece each day. They kept this up for two or three years. It was a labor of love as far as Rabbit Hill was concerned, but when the mortgage was finally paid, Robert Lawson never wanted to see another greeting card.

* From an article by Rose Henderson in the New York *Herald-Tribune,* November 30, 1930.

According to an article in *This Week*, the magazine section of the now-defunct New York *Herald-Tribune*, RL turned to etching when the bottom dropped out of the business world and the hand-painted Christmas card market in 1929. Be that as it may, in 1931 he received the John Taylor Arms Prize of the Society of American Etchers, and in 1932 he was asked to do the annual member's plate of the Society, shown on page one of this book. *The Art Digest* for November 15, 1932, carried a reduction of "We Fix Flats" with the comment that it was "characteristic of Lawson's well-known style and highly fanciful subject matter," and quoted the society's president, John Taylor Arms to the effect that "Lawson has explored an entirely new field of subject matter and one untouched by any other etcher in this country — the field of gnomes and fairies, of elves and goblins and sprites, of the cluricaune, the leprechaun and the merrow."

Meanwhile his exploration of this new field, and also his illustrations for Carl Sandburg's "Rootabaga Stories" that ran in a woman's magazine, *The Designer,* had led to his commission to illustrate *The Wee Men of Bally-wooden.* Most of his work after that followed the course which the present book has attempted to chart. Before the decade was out he was not so bothered by one of his pet aversions, that of "never having any money," nor had he need to work under such forced draft as to illustrate nine books in one year, which he did in 1937. By the end of the next decade he was illustrating only his own writing and was coming perilously close to the Utopia he said he wanted, being able to live on the royalties of a perpetually selling book — if you read "book" in the plural. He died in May 1957, the year after Mrs. Lawson died. His last published book, *The Great Wheel,* was still on press, and he had not finished his pencil sketches for a small whimsy, *Why Bats Are,* which he was playing with because, he confessed, he was too tired to undertake a longer, more ambitious project proposed by one of his editors.

RL had reason to be tired. He usually worked from nine to five or six every day, including Sundays and holidays, with brief intervals for gardening or garden watching, and in later years short breaks in Nantucket or the Berkshires or Virginia between jobs. Even these would be shortened by the intrusion of new ideas for new jobs and impatience to get at them.

Helen Dean Fish, his Lippincott editor, writing in *The Horn Book,* and Arthur Bartlett in *This Week* both tell RL's story demonstrating the soundness of children's criticism, though one says it was a boy, the other a girl who declared, after looking at an exhibit of book illustrations, "I like *his* best, because he draws them up nice and neat, and you can tell what they mean."

His methods of achieving this successful communication varied somewhat, although not fundamentally. He always depended on a precise line, but he experimented occasionally with the technique of drawing that line. His first books were done in very fine pen and ink, even sometimes with diluted ink. Because of the difficulty in securing satisfactory reproduction of such delicate lines, he began to use a somewhat coarser pen and then added the brush and black tempera of *Ferdinand* and *Mr. Popper*. He followed this with a rubbed and brushed Woolf pencil technique, which he described: "As far as I know, [it was] a development of my own. . . . I found that it [Woolf pencil] could be rubbed with a brush to give a tone which is easily picked off with a kneaded rubber for lights. A very sharp point, used almost like a pen, gives definition and textures. The whole process consists of an endless series of drawing, brushing, picking out lights with the rubber, over and over again, finally fixing and picking out the highlights with white tempera or by scraping with a knife." *

This was the process he used for *Pilgrim's Progress*, *Rabbit Hill* and other drawings in tone, necessitating offset halftone reproduction in order to avoid glossy paper or coarse halftone screens. Eventually, as offset techniques improved, his relatively fine pen line and tempera, such as the illustrations for *Mr. Revere* and *Captain Kidd*, were also reproduced by offset instead of letterpress, but by offset line rather than halftone, in order to achieve the clean line and solid blacks he insisted upon.

Concerning his methods of illustration beyond his drawing techniques, Robert Lawson wrote an article for *Publisher's Weekly*, December 7, 1935, which the author of the above-mentioned article in *Art Instruction* quoted almost in full because it was so illuminating. It is excerpted here for the same reason: ". . . just what is meant by illustration — is it merely to do in pictures what the author has already done in words, or to go on and carry out the spirit and atmosphere the author can really only suggest? The infinite detail which it is possible to put in a drawing to enhance the scene would, if written, hopelessly retard the action and drama of the narrative. To my mind this is the true function of the illustrator. He must steep himself in the atmosphere of the book, and then transfer that feeling to his drawings. . . .

"How this is done cannot be explained any more than an actress can explain how she creates a character from the few words the playwright has put in her mouth. I can, however, explain the mechanics of going about the illustration of a book:

"First, the illustrator reads the manuscript once or twice, without any thought of definite illustrations — simply to see what it's all about and to gather the general atmosphere. Then he usually goes through it again, and picks out those incidents which simply demand to be illustrated, either

* Quoted in an unsigned article in *Art Instruction*, November 1938.

because of their dramatic or atmospheric qualities. Then he goes through it again, and, according to the number of drawings allowed by the publisher, either subtracts some or adds more to help carry out the action and spirit of the text.

"The next step, usually, is to make a dummy the exact shape and size of the book, and to plan, roughly, the drawings themselves in their proper sizes and places. Then, with the drawings in this tangible form, he goes through this dummy again, adding here, eliminating there, until the drawings would, taken by themselves and without text, give a very clear idea of the feeling and progress of the story. Then all that remains is . . . to do the individual drawings themselves.

"How do you know what to put in the drawings? . . . For my own part I can say that only twice in something over twenty years has a definite idea for a drawing come out of thin air by the process called inspiration. It has always come by sitting down with paper and a pencil and thinking about the subject; by scratching and rubbing out and starting again. Eventually some combination of scratches and smudges . . . will suggest an arrangement or a point of view, and from then on it is simply a problem of building this up and elaborating upon it until the desired result is attained. I should say, approached — it is never attained.

"The life of any illustrator, I am sure, is an endless process of observing and stowing away in some curious ragbag part of his mind all the thousands of ill-assorted facts and impressions that he will sometime be called upon to use. . . . The poor illustrator may, at any moment, be called upon to dive into his memory and produce — correctly and recognizably drawn — a coast guard cutter or a razor blade, an Egyptian princess, a Chinese junk, a Christmas tree with all its candles, a circus parade or a little girl eating spinach.

"In addition to the memory ragbag, he must also have at hand or know where to locate quickly a tremendous amount of data; costume, architecture, furnishings, anatomy of man, bird, beast and reptile; marine architecture, and a hundred other things, either in book form or in clippings filed away and classified. And no matter how much of this he may have some author or editor will demand details which just cannot be located. . . .

"It is perhaps this variety of problems, and the never-ending succession of new and different things to be done that make the profession of illustration so fascinating. The illustrator becomes immersed in a new book, and is practically away somewhere for two days, or a night, a week, or a month or more. He comes up for air, looks about a while, and then is gone again, into some new delirium of work. Hand in hand with the author he treads the far high fields of the imagination or penetrates the breathtaking realms of science or industry. Whether he is reliving the dark days of the Revolution, campaigning with Marlborough, or viewing with Melville or Stevenson new lands and strange seas, he is, for a while, living that life and seeing those scenes.

"That is why so many illustrators seem uninterested in minor politics and world movements, and advertising patter, and why they often forget to tie their shoe laces."

RL at Rabbit Hill

"Toward the end of a long job I always get a feeling that it's all a sort of dream and that no one could possibly have the faintest interest in what I'm doing." *

* Letter to editor which was received after May 2, 1941.

ACKNOWLEDGMENTS

THIS BOOK was made possible by Little, Brown and Company and the Viking Press, who opened to me their files of books and correspondence. The letters from which excerpts have been quoted were written by Robert Lawson to his editors at Little, Brown.

Other publishers of books illustrated by RL helped in the search for original printings and out-of-print books, notably J. B. Lippincott Company, who made available to me books from the old Frederick A. Stokes files as well as their own.

The Lynn, Massachusetts, Public Library gave me access to many books no longer available from their publishers. Others were generously supplied by the Hartford, Connecticut, Public Library. The Boston Public Library, the Lexington, Massachusetts, Public Library, the New York Public Library and the Library of Congress filled in the few gaps that were left. The breadth and continuity of the children's book collections in these libraries, as well as the quick response of the librarians, must be of huge assistance to all researchers.

Thanks are due also to the Free Library of Philadelphia, which houses the Frederick R. Gardner Collection of original drawings and etchings by Robert Lawson, for making available the two etchings chosen for this book.

The author acknowledges with gratitude permission to reprint illustrations from the following specific sources:

Peik, copyright 1932 by Barbara Ring; *Haven's End,* copyright 1933 by John P. Marquand, copyright © renewed 1961; *Slim,* copyright 1934 by William Wister Haines, copyright © renewed 1962; *Mr. Popper's Penguins,* copyright 1938 by Florence Atwater, Doris Atwater, and Carroll Atwater Bishop, copyright © renewed 1966; *Ben and Me,* copyright 1939 by Robert Lawson, copyright © renewed 1967 by John W. Boyd; *Prince Prigio,* copyright 1942 by Little, Brown and Company, copyright © renewed 1970; *Watchwords of Liberty,* copyright 1943, © 1957 by Robert Lawson, copyright © renewed 1971 by Nina Forbes Bowman. All the foregoing published by Little, Brown and Company. Reprinted by permission of the publisher.

The Treasure of the Isle of Mist by W. W. Tarn. Copyright 1920 by W. W. Tarn, copyright renewed 1947. Reprinted by permission of G. P. Putnam's Sons.

Acknowledgments

The Wee Men of Ballywooden by Arthur Mason. Copyright 1930 by Arthur Mason, copyright © renewed 1958 by Mrs. Arthur Mason. Published by Doubleday & Company. Reissued by The Viking Press.

The Horn of the Moon and *The Roving Lobster,* both by Arthur Mason. Both copyright 1931 by Arthur Mason. Both copyright © renewed 1958 by Mary Frank Mason. Published by Doubleday & Company.

The Unicorn with Silver Shoes by Ella Young. Copyright 1932 by Ella Young, copyright © renewed 1959 by Jane R. Thompson. Used by permission of the publisher, David McKay Company, Inc.

Drums of Monmouth by Emma Gelders Sterne. Copyright 1935 by Dodd, Mead & Company, Inc., copyright © renewed 1963. Used by permission of Dodd, Mead & Company, Inc.

The Golden Horseshoe by Elizabeth Coatsworth. Copyright 1935 by The Macmillan Company, copyright © renewed 1962. Used by permission of The Macmillan Company.

The Hurdy-Gurdy Man by Margery Bianco. Copyright 1936 by Oxford University Press. Illustration copyright © renewed 1964 by John W. Boyd for the estate of Robert Lawson.

Seven Beads of Wampum by Elizabeth Gale. Copyright 1936 by Elizabeth Gale, copyright © renewed 1964. Reprinted by permission of G. P. Putnam's Sons.

The Story of Ferdinand by Munro Leaf. Copyright 1936 by Munro Leaf and Robert Lawson, copyright © renewed 1964 by Munro Leaf and John W. Boyd. Reprinted by permission of The Viking Press, Inc.

Four and Twenty Blackbirds selected by Helen Dean Fish. Copyright 1937 by J. B. Lippincott Company, copyright © renewed 1965 by Emily P. Street. Reproduced by permission of J. B. Lippincott Company.

I Hear America Singing collected by Ruth A. Barnes. Copyright 1937 by Holt, Rinehart and Winston, Inc., copyright © 1965 by Ruth A. Barnes. Reproduced by permission of Holt, Rinehart and Winston.

The Story of Jesus by Walter Russell Bowie. Copyright 1937 by Charles Scribner's Sons, renewal copyright © 1965 by Walter Russell Bowie. Reproduced by permission of Charles Scribner's Sons.

Under the Ten of the Sky edited by John Brewton. Copyright 1937 by The Macmillan Company, copyright © renewed 1965. Used by permission of The Macmillan Company.

Wind of the Vikings by Maribelle Cormack. Copyright 1937 by Appleton-Century Company. Illustration copyright © renewed 1965 by John W. Boyd for the estate of Robert Lawson.

One Foot in Fairyland by Eleanor Farjeon. Copyright 1938 by Frederick A. Stokes Company. Illustrations copyright © renewed 1966 by John W. Boyd for the estate of Robert Lawson.

Acknowledgments

Wee Gillis by Munro Leaf. Copyright 1938 by Munro Leaf and Robert Lawson, copyright © renewed 1966 by Munro Leaf and John W. Boyd. Reprinted by permission of The Viking Press, Inc.

Pilgrim's Progress by John Bunyan, retold by Mary Godolphin. Copyright 1939 by Frederick A. Stokes Company, copyright © renewed 1967 by John W. Boyd. Reproduced by permission of J. B. Lippincott Company.

Just For Fun. Copyright 1940, © 1968 by Rand McNally & Company. Used by permission of Nina Forbes Bowman.

They Were Strong and Good. Copyright 1940 by Robert Lawson, copyright © renewed 1968 by John W. Boyd. Reprinted by permission of The Viking Press, Inc.

Aesop's Fables retold by Munro Leaf, published by The Heritage Club. Copyright © 1941, 1969 by The George Macy Companies, Inc., New York, and used by arrangement with the publisher.

The Story of Simpson and Sampson by Munro Leaf. Copyright 1941 by Munro Leaf and Robert Lawson, copyright © renewed 1969 by Munro Leaf and John W. Boyd. Reprinted by permission of The Viking Press, Inc.

Adam of the Road by Elizabeth Janet Gray. Copyright 1942 by Elizabeth Janet Gray and Robert Lawson, copyright © renewed 1970 by Elizabeth Janet Gray and John W. Boyd. Reprinted by permission of The Viking Press, Inc.

The Crock of Gold by James Stephens. Copyright © 1942, 1970 by The Limited Editions Club, New York, and used by arrangement with the publisher.

The Little Woman Wanted Noise by Val Teal. Copyright 1943, © 1971 by Rand McNally & Company.

Rabbit Hill by Robert Lawson. Copyright 1944 by Robert Lawson, copyright © renewed 1972 by John W. Boyd. Reprinted by permission of The Viking Press, Inc.

At That Time by Robert Lawson. Copyright 1947 by Robert Lawson. Reprinted by permission of The Viking Press, Inc.

The Great Wheel by Robert Lawson. Copyright © 1957 by Robert Lawson. Reprinted by permission of The Viking Press, Inc.

Robbut by Robert Lawson. Copyright 1948 by Robert Lawson. Reprinted by permission of The Viking Press, Inc.

Smeller Martin by Robert Lawson. Copyright 1950 by Robert Lawson. Reprinted by permission of The Viking Press, Inc.

The Tough Winter by Robert Lawson. Copyright 1954 by Robert Lawson. Reprinted by permission of The Viking Press, Inc.

H. L. J.

BOOKS ILLUSTRATED BY ROBERT LAWSON

Atwater, Richard and Florence. *Mr. Popper's Penguins.* Little, 1938.

Barnes, Ruth. *I Hear America Singing.* Winston, 1937.

Bates, Helen Dixon. *Betsy Ross.* Whittlesey, 1936.

———. *Francis Scott Key.* Whittlesey, 1936.

Bianco, Margery Williams. *The Hurdy-Gurdy Man.* Oxford, 1933.

Bowie, Walter Russell. *The Story of Jesus.* Scribner, 1937.

Brewton, John E., editor. *Gaily We Parade.* Macmillan, 1940.

———. *Under the Ten of the Sky.* Macmillan, 1937.

Bunyan, John. *Pilgrim's Progress.* Retold by Mary Godolphin. Lippincott, 1939.

Chester, George R. *The Wonderful Adventures of Little Prince Toofat.* McCann, 1922.

Clemens, Samuel L. *The Prince and the Pauper.* Winston, 1937.

Coatsworth, Elizabeth. *The Golden Horseshoe.* Macmillan, 1935.

Cormack, Maribelle. *Wind of the Vikings.* Appleton-Century, 1937.

Dickens, Charles. *A Tale of Two Cities.* Ginn, 1938.

Farjeon, Eleanor. *One Foot in Fairyland.* Stokes, 1938.

Fish, Helen Dean. *Four and Twenty Blackbirds.* Lippincott, 1937.

Forester, C. S. *Poo-Poo and the Dragons.* Little, 1942.

Gale, Elizabeth. *Seven Beads of Wampum.* Putnam, 1936.

Gray, Elizabeth Janet. *Adam of the Road.* Viking, 1942.

Haines, William Wister. *Slim.* Little, 1934.

Hall, William. *The Shoelace Robin.* Crowell, 1945.

Lang, Andrew. *Prince Prigio.* Little, 1942.

Lawson, Robert. *At That Time.* Viking, 1947.

———. *Ben and Me.* Little, 1939.

———. *Capt. Kidd's Cat.* Little, 1956.

———. *Country Colic.* Little, 1944.

———. *Dick Whittington and His Cat.* Retold by Robert Lawson. Limited Editions Club, 1949.

———. *Edward, Hoppy and Joe.* Knopf, 1952.

———. *The Fabulous Flight.* Little, 1949.

———. *The Great Wheel.* Viking, 1957.

———. *I Discover Columbus.* Little, 1941.

————. *Just for Fun.* Collected stories and verse; no editor given. Rand, McNally, 1940.

————. *McWhinney's Jaunt.* Little, 1947.

————. *Mr. Revere and I.* Little, 1953.

————. *Mr. Twigg's Mistake.* Little, 1947.

————. *Mr. Wilmer.* Little, 1945.

————. *Rabbit Hill.* Viking, 1944.

————. *Robbut: A Tale of Tails.* Viking, 1948.

————. *Smeller Martin.* Viking, 1950.

————. *They Were Strong and Good.* Viking, 1940.

————. *The Tough Winter.* Viking, 1954.

————. *Watchwords of Liberty.* Little, 1943.

Leaf, Munro. *Aesop's Fables:* A New Version. Heritage, 1941.

————. *The Story of Ferdinand.* Viking, 1936.

————. *The Story of Simpson and Sampson.* Viking, 1941.

————. *Wee Gillis.* Viking, 1938.

Marquand, John. *Haven's End.* Little, 1933.

Mason, Arthur. *From the Horn of the Moon.* Doubleday, 1931.

————. *The Roving Lobster.* Doubleday, 1931.

————. *The Wee Men of Ballywooden.* Doubleday, 1930. Reissued by Viking, 1952.

Potter, Mary A. *Mathematics for Success.* Ginn, 1952.

Ring, Barbara. *Peik.* Little, 1932.

Robinson, Tom. *Greylock and the Robins.* Viking, 1946.

Stephens, James. *The Crock of Gold.* Limited Editions Club, 1942.

Sterne, Emma Gelders. *Drums of Monmouth.* Dodd, 1935.

————. *Miranda Is a Princess.* Dodd, 1937.

Stratton, Clarence. *Swords and Statues.* Winston, 1937.

Tarn, W. W. *Treasure of the Isle of Mist.* Putnam, 1934.

Teal, Val. *The Little Woman Wanted Noise.* Rand, McNally, 1943.

Young, Ella. *The Unicorn with Silver Shoes.* Longmans, 1932. Reissued by McKay, 1957.

Note: This bibliography has been checked with the excellent one prepared by Annette H. Weston for her article on Robert Lawson in *Elementary English,* January 1970. It differs only in minor corrections of titles and dates, and in the omission of translations and two titles which could not be verified as illustrated by Lawson. A text edition of *A Tale of Two Cities* has been added.

INDEX OF TITLES
REPRESENTED IN THIS BOOK